Raising
Someone Else's
Child

Melissa Euton

WORKBOOK PRESS LLC
187 E Warm Springs Rd,
Suite B285, Las Vegas, NV 89119, USA

Website: https://workbookpress.com/
Hotline: 1-888-818-4856
Email: admin@workbookpress.com

Ordering Information:
Quantity sales. Special discounts are available on quantity purchases by corporations, associations, and others.
For details, contact the publisher at the address above.

Library of Congress Control Number:
ISBN-13:   978-1-957618-92-0 (Paperback Version)
                978-1-957618-93-7 (Digital Version)

REV. DATE: 20/04/2022

Raising Someone Else's Child

Joy Rivers

Contents

Joy

March 1996, my husband and I had just completed our last foster-parenting class. We were so excited and overwhelmed; we felt so ready to start this new adventure. As we were leaving the class, we stopped to speak to Jenna, the social worker who was teaching the class. I asked, "When can we get started? How long does it take?"

Jenna was quick to point out that when they called me, a lot had happened with the family. A parent just lost their child due to a horrible event in their life. A child just lost their home, friends, and parents and maybe even the school that they love.

Wow, what was I thinking! I felt so bad. How was it that I never thought of what the child was going through? I guess I never thought of it that way. I was just thinking of how happy I would be to get a new child to be a part of our life. It was all about me. I was so thankful for that moment because as each child entered our home, I reminded myself of all the things they just lost.

March 15, we received our first placement. Now let me just say that we went from two children to five in the blink of an eye! Three boys—it really made you want to pull your hair out. It was that type of craziness. It never crossed my mind that these children wouldn't be raised the way I would raise a child. It took everything we had to offer for about a month to tame these boys.

The three boys were with us for four months. The first hour they were with me, I had to take them to the local Kmart to get clothing for them.

Lesson 1—most of the time, the children come with absolutely nothing but the clothes on their back. I had my two children with me, and as soon as we entered the store, all hell broke loose! They started running and hiding in the clothes racks. My two children were with me, and they looked at me in complete and utter shock. I said to my oldest, "You go get that one." And to my youngest, "Go get the youngest of the three, and I will grab the oldest one." The time we spent in the store seemed like an eternity. We were exhausted when we got home. My daughter asked, "Mom, how long are they staying?" I was wondering about that myself and at the same time thinking that I had made the biggest mistake of my life.

These three would come to get something to eat, and it would be an all-out war! They would bloody the other one's nose if that was what it took to eat first. Of course, my kids kept their distance, not understanding what in the world was going on. My husband and I would remind them daily that they would get three meals a day at our house—and snacks, if they wanted. "Just tell us you are hungry." The day the boys were taken was partly due to them eating out of a trash can, and one of them ate glass.

We had a couple of friends that wanted to meet the boys and help with some things around the house. The weekend they came, we decided to order pizza. I went out to get it and came home to set it on the table. I asked all the children to wash their hands and get ready to eat. I stepped outside and told my husband and his friend to come and eat. I turned to go back in the kitchen, and my friend and I were in shock when the three boys were on top of the table and there was no pizza! No kidding! Not one slice. I just sat in the kitchen chair and didn't even know what to say!

It took two months of working with them, and we finally all learned to gel as a team with everyday life. For example, we could go to the local Kmart and get what we needed and not hide in the clothes rack. We could go to dinner and leave with people saying, "What a lovely family you have." Our family had grown to love the three boys, despite the fact that they were rotten to the core.

The day came that Jenna called and said they had court. The boys were going home! I had all kinds of feelings going on; my feelings were all over the place. I felt a little downhearted at first, but I was also very excited for the boys to be reunited with their mother. When they got home from school and realized they were leaving, they felt confused and hurt to see their bags packed. I knew then I had to express to them that they were getting to not only go see but live with their real mom. The youngest boy was three. He had asked, "When will we come back?" I told him that even though I enjoyed them being a part of our family, he and his bothers would be staying with their mom full-time now, but not to worry. Due to the reasons he was removed in the first place, it was understandable that he was on edge.

The boys were afraid to go home, thinking that the same men that their mom would let sexually abuse them for drugs would still be there. Maybe they wouldn't get to eat like they did with us. Yes, you heard me right. Their own mother would pimp them out to nasty old men so that she could get drugs without paying.

I now wished I hadn't taken the fight and animallike behaviors out of them. Would they be able to survive? Would they fight like hell to get away from these men? So much was running through my mind.

I had spoken to their mother, and we agreed to meet after. My husband came home so that he could say goodbye. The evening came faster than expected, and it was time to say goodbye. I felt very emotional at this moment, but I knew that they would be okay. I kept telling myself that, but the reality was that we never knew how things would turn out. This was the truth about all the kids who went home after being with us. We didn't get to know how their lives turned out. That was one of the negatives of being a foster parent.

Soon after that, we were getting children left and right. I have to admit I never said no; I was very passionate about helping the next child! I loved all kids going through my home, but my favorite type of child was a baby. I guess it was more of a treat, considering we only got children from the ages of three to eight. However, it soon became clear to me that even though I did love having a baby, I found it was a lot easier to care for the baby. And it was also very hard for me to give the baby back.

Our next placement was a four-month-old baby girl. Her mother didn't want her, so she had taken the baby to her daddy's house and set her in the driveway on a cold winter day. Daddy called social services and told them there was a baby in a car seat in his driveway and told them to come and get it! He left her outside until the worker came.

She was a precious baby, and we enjoyed her stay with us so much. I didn't want to let her go. I mourned for months after she left. It made me realize that even though I loved having a baby again, it was not something I could do over and over.

The next set of three boys would forever change our lives even though we would not realize it until seven years later. On July 31, they came to our house, and for the first time, I had a child older than my daughter—which we said we didn't want to do in the beginning. The worker asked that we take him for the weekend, so we agreed. As Monday came, we decided to keep the older boy. The middle child had a lot of anger, which he displayed over and over throughout the weekend, so we asked that he be moved instead. The older boy gelled with our son, like they had always been together. Seven years later, the two became our sons with our second adoption.

We had the boys a couple of years and found the oldest—along with his siblings—suffered tremendous sexual abuse. After six years, he would eventually sexually abuse one of our adoptive placements. I will talk about that later.

In the first few years, you wouldn't have ever guessed that he was so abused. We didn't know until one night when we had had a wonderful evening. He came in and asked my husband and me if we would like to have sex with him. I about lost it. I sat him down and told him that adults don't have sex with their children. He said, "Don't you love me?"

When I reported it to the social worker, all the children started talking. There were six altogether, and they began therapy.

Life was good right now. We were becoming a nice family with four children. The boys were becoming very close to my children, and they were very happy.

So the joys of being a foster parent to me are as follows. First is when the worker calls and tells me it's a boy, a girl, or a sibling group. Second is when I watch the child grow and do well in school, in the community, and in life in general. Third, and most important, is when I have a meeting at social services and find out the parents love their children and are doing everything in their power to work through the system and reunite their family.

That is the real joy because that is the main goal of foster-parenting. As you get more and more kids and hear their terrible stories, well, we tend to forget that because it is easier to feel they don't deserve another chance.

Love Unconditionally

It came easy for my husband and me to love a child that was not ours by birth. We love kids and felt that we had a lot of love to share.

For me, I truly felt that I wanted to give back. My biological father was not in my life, but *my daddy* raised me with an unconditional love. He was there for me through everything. I am truly a daddy's girl. To this day, my daddy is my rock. He is always there even if it's just to hear about my day.

My dad adopted me when I was young, and I have always wanted to give back to a child the way he did for me. I think back now, and if I only had one wish in this world, it would be that he was my biological father. He has never treated me any different, but I still wish it were so.

So when a child would come in our home and was so hard and didn't want our love back, I did my best to change that. Over the twenty-two years that we have been in this, there are days we go to bed feeling so much pride and happiness. Then there are the nights we go to bed in tears because no matter what we try to do, they don't want or will not accept what we have to offer.

I have to tell about a few of the kids we had that truly left us with happy memories. We were blessed because we were privileged to know them. I know that God placed each and every child with us. There were some we could not help, but we hope we made an impression on them.

The first child that we will never forget was Shay. I was on my way to a Bible school program that my kids were in, and they were already at the church. A social worker called. She asked, "Will you take an eighteen-month-old little girl and her brother who is three? By the way, they are African American." I said, "Sure, but I need to leave shortly." The worker said, "I will be right there. Please wait for me!"

She arrived shortly with these two cuties, until they spoke! Ms. Shay was eighteen months old, and she came walking around my wraparound porch, grinning. She looked up at me while, at the same time, smacking my leg with the diaper she was carrying. The words that came out of her mouth were as plain as day: "I just shit. Change my ass!" Wow, I was about to collapse on the porch. One, she was so tiny, and two, the words were so plain and correctly put!

I changed her, and once the paperwork was done, off we went to the Bible school program. I got in the church house and made sure I sat in the back. Almost as soon as I sat down with my three small children, the preacher came to shake my hand, and he then asked me if the children could come to the front and join in. I answered very quickly, "No!" I explained I literally just got them, and they had never been to church! That was putting it nicely. As soon as I had released those words from my mouth, the three-year-old boy ran up on stage, grabbed a microphone, and said the F-word. He said it not once but over and over while the men in the church were chasing him, trying to get the microphone away from him.

After that, I was sure that I would be asked to leave. To my surprise, they let us finish the service. As soon as the kids finished, I gathered them up and left. To the older ones' surprise, we had two more kids that night. The boy didn't stay long, but Shay stayed for a year and six months. She may have stayed longer. We asked to adopt her and were told no because of her race. I was told that the laws at the time didn't support an adoption out of one's race. It was probably eight months later that the laws changed.

She was full of life, and she also filled ours with many stories. One that pops in my mind is when we went to visit our family; we didn't have her but about two months. She was sitting on my grandma's lap, and she was so tiny in stature, more the size of a one-year-old. Grandma asked me, "Why didn't the worker have any white kids for me?" Well, I guess Grandma thought she was too little to know what she was talking about; but long before I could answer, Shay looked at

Grandma and called her a bitch. I scolded her and couldn't believe she knew what Grandma was saying.

There are many stories I can tell about her. We really wanted to adopt her. We loved her so much. She did, however, stop cussing and was so sweet and pretty. As I write this, Shay would be twenty-two years old now. I did see her once after she was adopted. She was about five years old, and I squatted down to her and said, "Hi, Shay, Shay." My heart was broken because she didn't remember me. This did allow me to let go. I realized she was okay, and I would be also.

Back to unconditional love. It was hard at times. We had 110 foster children in our twenty-two years. Some were so beaten and destroyed emotionally and physically. You never knew how they were going to react. My husband and I believed that if we loved them enough, taught them right and wrong, then with God's help, they would be okay.

That is not always the case! That is why there are therapeutic foster homes for the medically fragile. There are many different types of homes, and sometimes the worker may not know that a higher-level home is needed until you inform them of the problems you're having. So keep a good relationship with your workers and the chain of command.

We rarely gave up and asked a child to be moved. There were a few children that we did have to call a worker and ask that they be found a new placement, for fear that the child would hurt one of our children.

Mrs. Ruby is my mentor and dear friend, my go-to when I needed anything, no matter what it was. Mrs. Ruby once told me this: "When a child is disrupting your home, get them respite for the weekend and see how your family does. If the home is peaceful and you can relax, it is time for that child to go!" I would do that—and oh, how right she was!

Support System

You absolutely cannot do this without a support system. What may work for you may not be exactly what works for your spouse. My husband and I have lost friends and even some family. People don't understand why you are doing this to yourself. Sometimes you will even ask yourself the same question!

We had too many kids that varied in age: teens, preteens, and infants. The church that we attended for a year asked us to leave. Yes, you read that right. One day, the preacher paid me a visit at my home when my husband was at work, and he asked that we find another church. His reason was that they didn't have classes for all the children. I knew it was because we had all different races, and probably, age was a factor also.

Well, personally, I promised God daily that if he sent the children, I would teach them about him. So I was hurt and asked the so-called preacher to leave. I did tell him I would pray for him!

One time, my neighbor in Georgetown refused to pick me and my children up when our car broke down. The words she used were "I will not allow the black child in my car." She was at church every Sunday also; my prayer list was getting large.

For me, my support system is my older children, my parents, and my church. I also have friends who were foster parents. They help a lot because they can relate. Social Service workers were also a huge help to me until I moved to Texas. Here, once the child is adopted, they are yours and there is no help.

The most important is to make time for your spouse. If you two fall apart, so will the family. We make a point to set aside time for each other. We have had many trials—way too many to count.

My husband often says, "What we go through in a week would kill a normal person!" It was just last week that on Tuesday, our eighteen-year-old son was arrested. He was suspected of stealing at his job by fellow employees. Also on Tuesday, I had a meeting with the school on my nine-year-old to figure out what next year holds. She is moving up to the next school but has some difficulty with math. So as her mom, I was worried and happy for her all at the same time. On Wednesday, our twenty-two-year-old son's girlfriend came to me. She was pregnant. The same day, my twenty-one-year-old son told me that he liked doing marijuana—that's why he couldn't get a job. On Thursday, our twenty-three-year-old daughter let me know that she was working this weekend and needed me to babysit. And let's not forget Friday. I had to take my thirteen-year-old to Houston to get the second surgery. I forgot about Monday, when the police showed up to tell me my dog got out of the fence and I needed to get him. So, needless to say, it was a very stressful week!

I almost naturally call my mom first. I also talk to my daughter Dawn, and she gives me a sibling's perspective. My husband and I go to bed sometimes so stressed we barely talk. We try to talk it out so we can at least get some sleep.

There are those kids that will make everything seem to have purpose and reason for why we put ourselves through this. Our nine-year-old is one of those kids. She never gets in trouble. She always tries to please people in general. She comes and tells us we are the best parents ever, and that she loves us. She is the one that keeps us going. We love all our children. We tell them that our relationship is like a bank; there are deposits and withdrawals. You can't keep taking withdrawals if you never make a deposit.

I am close with the schools. With the technology today, teachers and staff are just a text away. My job is always centered on my children and their schedule. My jobs have always been family-first orientated. Last but not least, my neighborhood. My neighbors are awesome. They help me anytime I ask. They watch out for my kids, making sure they are safe.

The saying "It takes a community to raise a child" is so true. I could not do this without my community and support systems in place.

Make time for you and your spouse. And if there are biological children, keep them well informed, and let them know they are no less important. I always told mine that these children need a family, and I tried to consult them before any changes ever happened.

Most of our children have grown up and are doing jobs that are giving back to people and their communities. I noticed our boys often date girls from broken homes and are always trying to fix their problems. I raised my children to break the cycle of broken homes and to do their best to have a productive life, take care of family and community, and give 100 percent at all times.

It is heartbreaking when my children do give it their all, and the person they picked doesn't have the same outlook on life. My son is ex-military and has a job with the FBI. He holds two jobs, and his fiancée took their baby girl and left him. He is a hardworking and wonderful dad, but I guess that is not good enough. This, I know, breaks his heart. He wants a family and loves his daughter very much. He never wanted to be an absentee father.

We don't always have a choice on how life will turn out. All we can do is give it 100 percent all the time and pray God will lead and guide our lives.

Adventure

One thing stupid people in our society always asked us is how much money we get for those kids. Well, social services do vary from state to state, but I will tell you right now. It takes everything they give you to raise them.

We always treated our foster children just like our own. Most of the time in Kentucky, the children came with nothing. So they would get a voucher for Kmart. I would get their underwear, socks, pajamas, and stuff, no matter the name brand. Then we would go to the outlet malls and get their clothes and shoes. If my kids wore Nike, so did they. I tried to make them feel good about themselves. Ask yourself this. When you go out of the house looking good, does it change the way you feel?

We also took vacations with the whole family. When we lived in Kentucky, for instance, we went to Niagara Falls along with another couple that foster-parented with us. They were from there and asked us to go. They had a family member that worked at a hotel, and all together, with both families, we took eighteen people.

They showed us around Buffalo, New York, and Niagara Falls on both sides. It was so much fun that we went back several times. We also went to South Carolina to see Dale Earnhardt. We were also able to take the kids through and see Dale and Dale Jr. We did that several times, and we went to Ohio to visit family.

We also would buy things for the kids to do, like trampolines, bicycles, and toys in general. One year, we put in an aboveground pool. We had a lot for them to do, and we liked to entertain.

Just taking the kids out to eat was at least $150 to $200. I did quit my job by this stage in our life to keep up with the busy schedule. We averaged twelve kids most of the time. There were family visits and doctor appointments; mealtime alone was a job. All the baths and hygiene kept me busy at bedtime. I enjoyed every minute of it usually; at times, it was hectic. We kept a routine, which helps if you have one or twelve.

I made a point, whenever I could, to spend extra time with my two children. At one point, I had all the little ones in day care, and the older ones went to school while I homeschooled my two, which allowed me to spend some extra time with just them.

It was just the other day when my daughter Dawn—who is about to have her own child—said, "I want to stay home with my baby the first few years and be there once they do get home from school." I told her I was glad she felt that way, but she had always went to day care, and it wasn't until she was older that I was home with them. So I guess I had done a good job of making them feel as if I was there for them.

I currently drive a school bus in Texas. My boss was so good to me that he made a route for me that included taking my two children who had issues to school. I am the first one they see as they go to school and as soon as they get on the bus to go home. I am also free during the day to spend time with the grandbabies when my adult children are off to work, and my date day with my husband is on Fridays.

My husband and I have been on many adventures through our life together. We started out with a three-bedroom house and one beautiful girl and one handsome boy. Life was great, and when we left Ohio and moved to Kentucky, we started a new one.

We were brand-new to the area and knew no one except the people we worked with. Once I started working, I had found an after-school program for Dawn. Little did I know it would change my life forever. The after-school program was where I met Mrs. Ruby. She and I would talk, and she helped me learn the community and make new acquaintances.

Mrs. Ruby was also a foster parent, and she began to tell me about it as I would ask her question after question. One day, she said, "You and your husband should be foster parents." And the rest is history; we had 110 foster children between Kentucky and, later, Ohio.

After years of kids coming and going and all the terrible and sad stories, we wanted out. I would call the caseworker and say I was done and wanted to quit, and before you knew it, they would call and say, "We have no one else." I, of course, said yes most of the time.

My husband and I talked and decided: no more foster-parenting! Well, God wasn't finished with us yet. I couldn't sleep, and I would pray, "God, we fostered all these kids and adopted three and had guardianship of one from Kentucky. What more do we need to do?"

Well, the sleepless nights continued and went on for months. I was on the computer one night, writing this book, and an ad popped up about adoption. There are five hundred thousand children in the United States alone that are looking for their forever families.

I began to become obsessed with looking at adoption sites at night when I couldn't sleep. I prayed, "Lord, if this is what we are supposed to do, then please show me and show my husband too."

Well, he began to work on Leonard, and I just kept looking, though I didn't know what I was looking for exactly. One night, at two in the morning, this set of four boys seemed to jump off the screen at me. They were in Austin, Texas. The website— if you would like to check it out—is called Texas Adoption Resource Exchange, or TARE for short.

They looked and sounded rotten, but God told me they were the ones to apply for, so I did! I went to bed, and I couldn't hold it. I woke my husband up and said, "I found the kids that God has led me to!" I then rolled over and slept like a baby that night and every night after that.

Well, the caseworker called a few days later and said that they matched us to the boys. I thought, *No surprise. That's how my God works.* She told me to get in touch with my local agency and let them know they would be sending the paperwork to get things started. So I did, but they didn't seem too excited.

Time went by, and I had already started a redo on their new room, which was funny. Our friends would come to visit, and they would ask what I was doing, and I told them we were getting four boys from Texas. They didn't believe me; my husband was even wondering if I had lost my mind. I had never been so close to the Lord. I knew I was getting those boys!

The caseworker called and let me know that it had been two weeks, and the agency wasn't doing anything. She said, "Go talk to them and tell them it would be well worth their while to do the mountain of paperwork. Texas will compensate them well."

Needless to say, I got in my car and went straight over and talked to the main man. I explained what she said, and he went and got the *box* of paperwork. He said, "Do you see this? We are busy. We don't have time to go through all this." I asked him to call the worker right now while I was there. He did. I don't know what she said to him, but a week later, we were talking to the worker, and the boys were going to be ours!

It was actually a couple of months until everything went through interstate compact because we were in another state. Then the worker called to set up a date to come spend three days with the boys in Austin and bring them home. Then once they lived with us for six months, the adoption would go through in Ohio.

We were all set and on a plane to Texas to meet our boys. The kids back home were excited also. We had our two children along with our foster daughter Cindy, who, to this day, is still a part of our family. Our son Dillon, whom we had adopted, was twelve then. Dillon was one of our first foster children in Kentucky, and after seven years, we were able to adopt him and his brother. So there were four at home and two grown children at the time we were getting the boys.

I can honestly tell you that when we met them, it was not love at first sight. They were so hyper and rotten to the core. We took them to McDonald's, and the oldest and two younger ones latterly climbed the wall outside. I hate for people to drink after me, and they would run to the table and drink out of my drink. The youngest, Brad, wet his pants during the meal. We spent the day with them and then fell in the bed at the hotel, wondering, *Can we do this?*

By day 3, we did decided we would love these boys and welcome them into our family. They were ten, nine, six, and five.

They were excited but scared, now thinking like them. They were about to board a plane with two people who were now Mom and Dad and go halfway across the country. Wow. That's a lot to take in all in three days.

As of today, we have our two by birth and fourteen adopted children. Cindy has been with our family since she was fourteen. Cindy even moved to Texas with us and is married and doing well.

We had two more adoptions out of Texas. Seven months later, after getting the boys, we were asked if we would take a group of four siblings. There were three girls and one boy; we said sure. Then after I became an adoption coordinator for our local agency, we took our son home from Texas.

As far as adventures go, my husband and I feel we have always been on one since we met. I love him and can't think of anyone better to ride with on this roller coaster that we personally call life.

Growth

I know my husband and I have grown stronger and wiser through the years. It has also been brought to our attention that life is rough and not every family lives this fairy-tale life.

I have seen many children with broken bones from parents throwing them as babies for crying too much. I have heard children cry all night because they want their mommy. I have seen teen girls have sex with many boys at a time because they were gang-raped. And to this day, they couldn't cope with what happened and have lost their children; so the cycle repeats itself.

You can't do anything but grow. There is nothing you can do but be strong and try to show these kids the right way. We pray that God will watch over each and every one of them.

I have seen great things also—kids that come to us in such a broken state and yet leave happy and with real goals in life. One thing that took us time to learn is that you can't help them all. No matter how much you pray, how much you love and care for them, it doesn't change what they do. They go right back to the vomit that they came from in the first place.

I have been to many graduations! I am so proud of those who have finished school. I have attended many weddings and even thrown several.

We presently have eight grandchildren and have three on the way! So, most of the time, we don't do anything without doing it big!

We don't get to see all of them often, for three of our kids don't live in Texas. It's a whole different world with grandbabies. I love them to pieces, and they are always depositing in the bank we call life. I know that one day, they will need withdrawals—but for now, we will enjoy!

I have watched my children that come from broken homes be wonderful parents. I also have some that struggle; one of mine has even abandoned her child. For the life of me, I can't even possibly understand that. I would rather see her leave the child with her grandparents, where we know she is well cared for, than to have her drag the child all over the country while trying to figure out who she is. She may have been at a breaking point, and who knows what might have happened.

Yes, there are children whom we have raised, and once they are grown, they leave and have nothing to do with us or the rest of the family. That is hard to take sometimes, but it's the way they think.

Some even struggle year after year; you might wonder if it matters how old they were when we adopted them. I do think it matters. The ones that we struggled most with were those above the age of five at the time of their adoption. We had three that we had since they were two, and so far, two are at home still. They are thirteen and twelve years old at this time. My son that was in the marines and who is now working for the FBI is the other. We only adopted one that we had as a baby, and that would be our youngest daughter. She is nine at present.

She still has a way to go, but so far, she is a total blessing in our life. She keeps us going. The older siblings are still close to her; she is the cheerleader of the bunch.

Her growth has been nothing short of a miracle. Born in West Virginia with a meth addiction, she was so sick. She had a lot of food issues; her skin and respiratory problems were so severe that she was in the hospital many times. It took the first year to get through the medical conditions. Then we noticed she would not speak to anyone outside the home.

The first three years of school, she did not speak. They had a hard time because there were not many ways to measure what she knew. This year, she is in third grade and is doing awesome, as I said before. She is talking and getting straight As.

The principal said that she is their miracle child—a story of success. I am so proud of her, and believe me, it took each teacher and the staff to get her where she is today.

I also have my son who is thirteen; he was born with disabilities. He was one pound and six ounces with a cocaine addiction. They also later diagnosed him with fetal alcohol syndrome. At the time, he was a hot mess! He would steal daily, lie often, and would do anything he could get away with. He was in a behavior unit at school but went out for several classes; he got As. I would give you more of him, but we have yet to figure him out. I told all his teachers: "He is one of a kind. You will never meet anyone like him." He has had so much growth and is doing so well in school today that you wouldn't know it is the same kid. He has definitely grown; he is very loving and is one of those kids that will ask you how your day was. Then when you're not looking, he will take something! We love him. Life would not be the same without him.

I attended a meeting on him today, and he is doing awesome! He is out for all classes except math. He struggles with math, but it also allows him to have a safe place—a *base*, so to speak. It makes him feel safe.

So, on the subject of growth, I feel we do see growth. It just seems that sometimes, the bad outweighs the good. Please remember, if you choose to go down this path, make sure you are in it for the long haul. It will take a toll on you.

Anger

Today anger is all I feel!

My thirteen-year-old stole again! He just had surgery in Houston on his cleft palate; he was supposed to be taking it easy, but *no*! He climbed over my locked bedroom door to steal his dad's work computer. We were doing some remolding, so above the door, it was open. He downloaded games on it, which my husband's boss could see, and for which he could get fired. Do you think he cared? No!

Then my twenty-one-year-old daughter called from California and asked if—once she got rich and famous—she could get her daughter back. She left her daughter with her daddy's parents and moved to Florida. The reason she was asking was it had been a year now, and the court would give his family custody of the baby. I had to watch myself. I wanted to go off on her. I mean really!

Here we go back to another week filled with ups and downs. My Cindy called early this morning and let me know she was at the emergency room. She was pregnant again.

She had had three miscarriages and was scared because she was hurting so bad.

My nine-year-old prayed every night for months for her two sisters—our daughters Dawn and Cindy—who wanted to have a baby. Well, Cindy did become pregnant first; but sadly, she lost him at eleven weeks. Dawn still was pregnant, and so was Cindy, again. I just found out!

So here I had Rose who has a beautiful, smart, and healthy baby girl, but she gave her away and left, never to see her again. Then I had Cindy and her husband with their stable life, and they would love nothing more than to have a child.

I got angry, and I didn't understand where my kids were coming from. Her own parents abandoned her. What was she thinking? She knows exactly what that can do to a child.

It seemed like we were getting more and more bad days than good. It seemed that these kids just threw away their lives. Why? For the life of me, I can never understand. My husband and I are trying with all we've got to prevent this from happening!

There is a verse in the second book of Peter, where it talks about a dog turning to his own vomit again and the sow that was washed returning to wallow in the mire. We feel this is a true verse for the way some of the kids turned out. They have returned to the ways of their parents.

What can we do as parents? Part of me wants to say, "I will worry about my three little ones and not the rest of the craziness in my life." So once again, I air out all these to make you realize that it is not like they say in the foster-parenting classes. They can't begin to tell you what you will go through. I haven't even told you any stories behind my children. I have just told you what we lived through.

Most of the foster-parent classes are taught by people that are not parents themselves. They don't have a clue what it is like to be a parent, let alone a parent of a troubled child.

That brings me to the system, which is broken and messed up! We had a child that had mental issues. We were told he was a sociopath by three therapists. We tried for years to get help for him, and no help was given. We were even told, "You adopted him. It's your problem."

He put us through hell for eight long years. I can honestly say he enjoyed it. He reported us to social services and did crimes to get the police involved. Each week was a new thing. He ran away constantly. He also never finished school.

There was no helping him. We tried, and social services didn't help either. Once, when he was seventeen, he landed on the porch of a church that we attended for a while, and they made him a room and took him in. He and the preacher got along really well. Looking at him now, he should have been removed from his sibling group and adopted out by himself. He would have benefited from a single-parent family.

The problem is that we can't look into the future and know how it will turn out. I have people tell me that my own two kids could have turned out differently. This is true, which takes me back to the nature versus nurture principle—nature wins every time!

Frustration

Our family just decided to go out to dinner tonight; let me tell you what we had to go through before we left. First, our thirteen-year-old son couldn't just go to the car; he had to stand on the running board and jump up and down. So I corrected him!

Then our seventeen-year-old daughter was hanging out in the bathroom instead of leaving with her friend. We wanted to lock up the house before we left. She came out of the shower and had two handprints around her neck. I asked as we were all walking out the door, "What happened to your neck?" Her reply was "I got in a discussion with my friend!" My response was "really?" Then because of some recent events where she had been leaving the door unlocked, my husband checked the doors and windows. Guess what? No surprise— all the windows were unlocked! So people could sneak in, we guessed.

In our home, they all lied and made you think you were crazy—so you couldn't figure out what exactly happened. So we ended up just going to dinner, and then we came straight home.

I didn't understand why they always wanted to see what they could get over on you. Why can't we just enjoy going out to eat, grabbing a movie, and just having a normal night like any other family?

The feeling of frustration also came to my mind when you were dealing with the birth parents. You would have some that refused to do what they needed to do in order to get their child back. Why? I can't imagine not doing whatever was asked of me to get my children *back*. Nothing would stop me.

Yet time after time, the birth parents wouldn't even make it to a visit. As the foster mom, I never canceled a visit because I knew how important this was to the child. It was very hard to comfort a child when the parent didn't show.

Then there was the system that, at times, failed the child. I have seen children removed from their parents for some of the stupidest reasons. Once, I had two little boys in Kentucky that were removed because their parents were having sex and left the boys in the other room with their grandmother, who was in a wheelchair and couldn't attend to their needs.

When we went to court, the judge asked, "Would you have taken them if the parents were in the shower?" So he demanded that they be returned as soon as possible. I figured that out, so I already had them packed up, and they got to go home right then. After that, I never assumed that the parent was always wrong and social services was always right. Sometimes people just have situations where they need some help.

Frustration with the child was the hardest, when you couldn't fix what was wrong. You couldn't make Mom and Dad do what they were supposed to. It is hard every time they say goodbye at a visit. Think of when you go visit a loved one, and when the week is done, the goodbyes are the hardest part of the trip. To small children, they feel like it is forever—a long time between weekly visits.

Mourning

I promise this was, by far, the hardest for me; it's the reason I stopped foster-parenting. I had so many goodbyes that broke my heart.

Brittany, was placed at two month old then she left at eight months. I cried for at least two months. Shay, whom I had for eighteen months, can still bring out my tears today.

And there was John, whom I had for a couple of years, and I almost was able to adopt him. At the last minute, his parents came through for him. I did see John again a couple of years ago. He was seventeen. His worker said he was in a program in Houston and allowed us to visit him. We shared pictures with him and told him the story. His social worker said that he didn't do well growing up because she said he always felt we were his parents and we didn't want him. That alone broke my heart all over again. See, that was when social services felt it was best to give him back to his parents after two years. They messed him up, so it was not fair to him or us. He was in and out of care for years, and he was full of anger and so confused on his identity.

Jose, he was our boy. He came to us at twelve, and we loved him so much. He had been with us a year and was doing very well when our boy we had for six years molested a little girl that we had had for a while. Oh, what a nightmare. Social services said that if we were to continue to talk to him, then they would remove all the other children. We had a few days to think about it. They moved him to a group home. We thought about it, and we have had him and his brother for six years. The brother was two when he came. He knew nothing else but us. That would mean that Jose and the two little girls and another boy would have to go. The two girls, Lee and Jess, were in our home as an adoption placement. It was a huge decision, but it was one we had to make. They were all moved. I got a friend of mine to foster-parent, and she had just finished classes, so I worked it out that she take them all but Jose. He went to where his siblings were placed—also my friend.

We basically had had enough and decided to move to Ohio. Since the boys were placed with us for adoption, we waited till that was completed and moved. It was a fresh start for all of us; our older boy did well after therapy. We didn't live in Ohio long when Jose's father asked us to take guardianship of him. We did. At age nineteen, he moved back to Kentucky and died of a drug overdose. Jose was always torn between his life with us and his life with his dad.

Jess and Lee were babies, and after the abuse, they had to go, according to social services. It didn't hurt any less. We loved them even though we just had them under a year. It was really hard because they didn't understand what was happening.

Mac and Zac were two boys that came to me twice for placement; each time, they stayed for a year. They were so sweet and loving. They were so dirty when I got them. The social worker carried them in at two in the morning and laid them on my couch. I slept in the recliner, afraid they might wake up scared. I gave them a bath the next morning and discovered they had lice. I didn't realize they were white until after the third bath. Zac was the younger one, and he didn't like visits to his mom. So he and I had this thing. When he needed to stay with his mom for the weekend, I would give him fifty cents to get a soda out of the machine in his trailer park. He would then go to get it, and it would distract him until I could leave.

The last time I saw him, I let him know that he was going to be staying with his mom for good and that I would not be back. Zac said, "Mommy, that what you said last time!" I assured him I was not coming back and gave him his fifty cents. He got out of the van. I was fighting back the tears, and he ran toward the soda machine. I was getting their clothes out for his mom, and Zac was pulling on my shirttail: "Mom." I bent down to see what he wanted, and he said, "Mommy, keep my fifty cents for when you come back." With that big smile, he said, "You will be back."

Well, I am sorry to say he was right—his mom did mess up! But I was also right. I didn't come and rescue him. Social services removed them, but his mom had moved to another county. By the way, parents do this to avoid getting the kids removed. Since she did move, the boys were placed in that county. Zac's dad was able to get him, and Mac was put with foster parents. I found out from a worker friend of mine that Zac's dad molested him, and he was moved again. I was so mad. I had him for two years! Why didn't he get to come to me? I still had his fifty cents with his picture. I cried for months, wondering if he was somewhere wondering why I didn't come and get him.

I am crying now while writing this; all the feelings come back for all my babies out there who think I abandoned them.

This is a story that can fall under many of these chapters; frustration comes in because the system failed these boys! The parents should not be able to move and the worker places them in that county. Two years I had them, and they were under five! I was all they knew. Can you imagine what they were thinking, going to a new family?

I remind you that I had 110 children in foster care. Yes. For some, I was glad to see them go home to their family; some should never have. It is heartbreaking.

Hope

My hope for you is that you complete your classes and get the home study done. Then you will be on your way through this journey. I want you to keep an open mind. And please remember that even though the social workers have seen a lot, they cannot tell you what the child will bring to your home.

There is hope that I want to leave with you. I have had children come through here, and they are successful. Most of mine are also successful. I have a few that are making bad choices, but all in all, they have done well.

There are so many children that need our homes, so just keep an open mind. Some children come from sexual abuse, mental abuse, and physical abuse to things you can't even imagine.

Some children will come in calling you Mom and Dad from the start and be happy; others will resent you and think you're trying to take their parents' place. They don't understand that their parents messed up and you're just trying to help until they get to go home.

I always tried to be open-minded and very respectful to the parents, even if they were not. I did it for the children, not for the parents necessarily. The children watch our behavior, so be careful.

I have some that still keep in touch with me through Facebook or will call once in a while to catch up. Some have repeated the cycle of their parents and have their own kids in the foster-care system.

I want to go over my sixteen children and our foster daughter.

Our first adoption was our daughter, who is thirty-five. She was married; now they are divorced but remain best friends. They have three very smart and beautiful children. They live in Kentucky and are doing fine.

Our second adoption gave us our son who is thirty. He lives in Tennessee. He is doing fine, and he works in construction.

Our Cindy would be next. She is married and lives in Texas near us. They are doing well, and as of this writing, she has informed me that she is expecting.

Just one month behind her is our biological daughter Dawn, who is twenty-eight and pregnant with her first child. Her husband is a teacher at a local college.

Our son who is twenty-seven is next, and he is with one of our adopted daughters, who is now twenty-three. They have two beautiful children, and they bought a house nearby.

You did see that right. You may encounter your biological children being attracted to your adopted children. It was very hard for all of us to take at first, but they have been together for six years and are doing well.

Our son who was adopted with his older brother in the second adoption is next. He is out of the marines and currently works in Virginia. He met a girl there and didn't return to Texas due to his job and wanting to be close to her. He has two jobs, and they have a baby girl who is cute as a button!

Next would be our son who is twenty-four. He lives in Austin, Texas, where he chose to be close to his biological mother. He is doing well, as far as we know, and he comes home to visit once in a while.

Our son G-man is next. He is twenty-three and has an awesome girlfriend that we love. They bought their first home and are remolding it and are expecting a baby of their own.

Next is our daughter Rose; she is twenty-two. She has moved to California with dreams of becoming rich and famous. She has abandoned her daughter here in Texas.

Next is our son who is twenty. He lives here close by and is getting back on his feet after making some bad choices. He is a very hard worker—our go-to guy, especially when you want something clean!

Next is our son who is eighteen. He lives here at home and is a great kid. He recently made a bad choice (stealing at work) and is now facing charges. He has not let it stop him. He is back to work at the refineries and, hopefully, will not do it again. We can only hope that they learn from their mistakes.

Our next son is also eighteen. The boys are six months apart. He was a constant run and in trouble with the law. He took pleasure in reporting us to social services multiple times. We have no contact with him, and he is the son that lives at a local church.

Our daughter is seventeen, and she still lives at home. She is finishing her junior year of high school. Then we have our three smaller ones: they are thirteen, twelve, and nine.

So there you have it—our seventeen children. In summary, we have our two biological children and our foster daughter. Then we have adopted two sets of four, two sets of two, and two single adoptions.

As of today, we have eight grandchildren and three on the way! We have a busy and exciting life; my husband works full-time while I work part-time driving a bus. I had a bad day yesterday, and there are days I wonder why I put myself through this. Today is a new day. My grandbabies are supposed to come and visit, and my husband is fixing their teeter-totter. Lunch is all over. I am caught up with my chores; it's a good day for a great day!

The Bible says in the book of James, "He that has faith but does not have works—can that faith save him? If a brother or a sister is poorly clothed and lacking in daily food, and one of you says to them, 'Go in peace, be warmed and filled' without giving the things needed for the body, what good is that? So also faith by itself, if it does not have works, is dead."

Go and fulfill your calling!